T0328514

When the Sun turns Red

When the Sun turns Red

✿ ✿ ✿

*Women's Tears from a
Land in Despair*

Edited by Lilian Atanga and Sally Mboumien

SPEARS BOOKS
Denver, Colorado

Spears Books
An Imprint of Spears Media Press LLC
7830 W. Alameda Ave, Suite 103-247
Denver, CO 80226
United States of America

First Published in the United States of America in 2022 by Spears Books
www.spearsmedia.com
info@spearsmedia.com
@spearsbooks

Information on this title: www.spearsmedia.com/when-the-sun-turns-red
© 2022 Lilian Atanga & Sally Mboumien
All rights reserved.

ISBN: 9781957296043 (Paperback)
Also available in Kindle format

Cover photo: Johannes Plenio
Cover designed by D. Kambem
Designed and typeset by Spears Media Press LLC

Distributed globally by African Books Collective (ABC)
www.africanbookscollective.com

To all the women in Southern Cameroons especially displaced women and refugees across the world.

Contents

INTRODUCTION

Between 2019 and 2020, women of the coalition – South West North West Women's Taskforce, after different peace campaigns, from (public) lamentations to open letters, Twitter campaigns, Facebook campaigns, zoom conversation series with other Southern Cameroons women in the diaspora, chose to take an alternative format to express their pain and frustrations. These women choose poetry as a terse form of expression as actions and talking yielded minimal fruits.

Following an ongoing conflict in the English-speaking regions of Cameroon that erupted in 2017, and has witnessed severe and gruesome human rights violations, women working for peace under the umbrella of the South West North West Women Taskforce (SNWOT), decided to bring their perspective to the narrative by adding the women's voice through poetry. SNWOT is a coalition of women leaders and women led organizations within the English-speaking regions contributing significantly to end the ongoing conflict while ensuring women's meaningful participation in decision-making at all levels of the peace process. These women, since June 2018 have been carrying out nonviolent actions to communicate their stance on the conflict to all parties to the conflict and other national and international stakeholders. The attention given to these women's contributions were not encouraging making the need to rebrand their perspectives as voices in the conflict eminent. In the most authentic manner, these women inject a voice into the discourse of the conflict, a voice that echoes the often neglected third narrative which is a position many unarmed civilians find themselves in the whole saga. This poetic representation sought to balance the conversation on the conflict since it was continuously being discussed on the basis of power sharing and military actions with little or no focus on ensuring social justice and inclusion for all.

Ashuntantang and Tande in the introduction of their 2020 poetry anthology wrote:

To write is *to confront*
To write is to remember
To write is to resist
To write is to testify
To write is to heal

This collection is a true realization of the above as the women seek not only to confront or remember, resists, testify or heal, but also to represent their pain and frustrations as people living the conflict on a day-to-day basis within the North West and South West regions of Cameroon. The collection demonstrates a deeper experience and understanding of the dehumanizing circumstances in which people find themselves.

HISTORICAL UNDERPINNINGS

While Ashuntantang and Tande (2020) lay the historical background in their anthology, giving a synopsis of the conflict, other historians and social scientists have also explored the background to the armed conflict in the English-speaking regions of Cameroon, and here we note it is important to briefly explain some of the historical facts. With a colonial heritage, moving from the German colonizers in the late 19th century with the partition of Africa, to the English and the French seizing German colonies after the First World War defeat of Germany, splitting the German colony into two territories, and later eventually merging the English Southern Cameroons with the French Cameroon at independence, the English-speaking Cameroons have for over a century experienced different leadership. An eventual consequence of this is marginalization and discrimination from unity with the French Cameroons for over half a century. Ngoh (1999, 2019) has extensively explored the origins of the marginalization of former Southern Cameroonians (Anglophones). This marginalization is a product (perhaps) of their minority position in the united Cameroon, both in numbers (20% of population) and English language use. This has resulted in a fragmented, ruptured and subsequently abused heritage. In an effort to reclaim not only a threatened identity but a heritage that continually and progressively is experiencing erosion, a civil strike started in 2016 and escalated into an armed conflict in 2017. Multiple efforts to draw the attention of the government to a re-valorization of the Anglo-Saxon system of education and the common law legal system failed and an eventual degeneration to an armed conflict (Willis, Angove, Mbinkar, & McAulay, 2020, see also Ndofor & Ray 2022).

As a consequence, these English-speaking regions have been experiencing since 2017 traumatic and violent acts with women at the center of the conflict playing a significant role not only as victims, but also as actors and advocates in calling for a peaceful resolution of the conflict. Several women leaders after proposing possible ways of resolving the conflict, unfortunately have not been listened to and even when heard, their views have not been overtly adopted by many stakeholders. Initiatives put in place by the government of Cameroon like the Major National Dialogue to resolve this conflict have often side-lined women or brought them in to check boxes. Creating a space for these women to tell their perspective of the conflict, this poetry collection captures the untold sufferings and neglected expectations of women which the current media, peace processes, political and military actions take for granted.

THIS COLLECTION

Contributors to this volume have opted to tell their point of view through poetry because it enables them to speak up and speak out in ways that depict their needs and aspirations. This largely contributes to bridging the gap in representation as women from all walks of life had the opportunity to pen down their thoughts. The variance of poems in terms of form and style reflects the diversity of women with different educational, social, economic, and professional levels but with an utmost interest in including the pains and thoughts from these different women. They showcase the important role grassroots activism plays in contemporary peace-building strategies. It is worth noting that poetry as a genre to depict women not only as victims that need protection but to highlight their perspectives as change-makers, and as stakeholders with a voice, and diverse opinions/perspectives on varied issues.

Women's contributions to peace processes are often undermined as well as grossly under documented, hence, this collection advances grassroots activism in ways that might attract a global readership. Decision-making, reporting and peace settlements in particular usually exclude women although most decisions are made, or actions reported to ensure women's well-being. This collection brings to light the voices of these women leaders serving within grassroots communities. It is a strategic approach to showcase the power of inclusion in conflict management and transformation.

Worthy of note is the fact that most of the authors of these poems have never written a piece of poetry before. Some have just a basic notion of what the canons of poetry are. But all the authors know the power of expression, which digs deep into their pains, culminating in a cathartic release. For absence of voice and where to vent, women turn to art (Levi-Hazan & Harel-Shalev 2019) and poetry provides room for a brief and succinct representation of this pain.

This expression of pain is reflected in the everyday lives of these women for whom blood, death and burial are now everyday phenomena. Coming from a previously peaceful society and now compelled to take up the responsibility of digging graves and burying the dead, a hitherto male activity, the poems in this collection capture women's experiences, akin to the dirges that are customary in the traditional funeral art of most of the coastal, forest and Grassfields Bantu peoples (Finnegan 2012; Egbe 2019). These poems may thus be read as funeral songs.

Collectively, these poems consist of songs of sorrow, songs of pain, songs of love, songs of death, and songs of hope. They echo the cries of mothers, wives, daughters, and sisters. They reveal the cries of the rich and the poor. They express women's battle for peace, in an attempt to silence the guns. Yet they are also voices in the wilderness, drowned by the sound of battle. Poetry thus becomes their most viable weapon to fight the evil that has befallen their sons, husbands, fathers and brothers. They also decry the evil that has corroded womanhood – pushing some women to pick up arms.

We pitch this collection as an expression of art inspired by war, fear, pain and anger. Its form, not adhering to poetic canons would reflect the instability at the time of writing, the turbulence and the absence of rhythm. Whilst this collection is not the first piece of art in history inspired by war, it is special because it comes out as a *takumbeng* (Atanga 2010) – a women's secret society known for exorcising the evil that besieges the land. Crying and talking away the evil are harnessed as weapons, albeit in nonviolent ways – tools that are culturally available to the women.

FACEBOOK ADVOCACY AND HASHTAGS

At the end of each poem in this volume, women use different hashtags to highlight the issues at stake. This is in line with what Dadas (2017:17) calls hashtag activism, that is 'the attempt to use Twitter's [and other social media] hashtags to incite social change." This volume is a collation of the advocacy poetry and associated hashtags of the South West North West Women's Task force on Facebook at a specific point in time. Facebook, at the time served as the only platform or public space that these women could use without censure and free of physical violence (although it was not free from social media trolls). The Hashtags used at the end of their poems reflected the issues that preoccupied their activism at that time, including:

#snwot4peace
#WomenPeaceBuilders
#Talksnotblood

#Endanglophonecrises
#EnoughOfTheSuffering
#StopTheBurning
#TakeAPositiveAction
#InclusiveAndSincereDialogue
#CeasefireNow
#EndHostilitiesNow
#EducationNotGuns
#WeNeedPeace
#Pensnotguns

Social media provided visibility not only for women's activism but also for the conflict that provoked women's plight in Southern Cameroons

Lilian Atanga and Sally Mboumien

REFERENCES

Ashuntantang, J. &. Tande, D. (2020). *Bearing Witness: Poems from a Land in Turmoil.* Denver: Spears Media Press.

Atanga, L. L. (2010). *Gender, discourse and power in the Cameroonian parliament.* Bamenda: Langaa RPCIG

Dadas, C. (2017). "Hashtag Activism: The Promise and Risk of "Attention." in Walls, D. M., & Vie, S. (Eds.) *Social Writing/ Social Media: Publics, Presentations, and Pedagogies.* The WAC Clearinghouse; University Press of Colorado. https://doi.org/10.37514/PER-B.2017.0063

Egbe, M. (2019). Death, The Deceased and The Dead: Changing Trends in The Funeral Rituals of the Bayangi people of Cameroon. *Socio-antropología de la muerte: Nuevos enfoques en el estudio de la muerte*, 26.

Finnegan, R. (2012). *Oral literature in Africa.* Cambridge: Open Book Publishers.

Levi-Hazan, Y., & Harel-Shalev, A. (2019). 'Where am I in this story?'–listening to activist women writers. *Journal of Gender Studies*, 28(4), 387-401.

Ndofor, H. A., & Ray, C. A. (2022, May 22). *Cameroon: Africa's Unseen Crisis.* Retrieved from Foreign Policy: Africa Program: https://www.fpri.org/article/2022/05/cameroon-africas-unseen-crisis/

Ngoh, V. J. (1999). The origin of the marginalization of former Southern Cameroonians (Anglophones), 1961-1966: An historical analysis. *Journal of Third World Studies*, 16(1), 165-185.

Ngoh, V. J. (2019). *Cameroon 1884-Present (2018): The History of a People.* Limbe: Design House. Revised and Updated Edition

Willis, R., Angove, J., Mbinkar, C., & McAulay, J. (2020). 'We Remain Their Slaves': Voices from the Cameroon Conflict. *The Cameroon Conflict Research Group, University of Oxford Faculty of Law Working Paper.* https://www.law.ox.ac.uk/sites/default/files/migrated/ssrn-id3576732-1.pdf

Sirri Cynthia Wakuna

Tears of a Sister

In my land which I love
The mornings were filled with life, laughter, and peace.
As I walked through the streets, I smiled at the soothing voices of children
Singing and chanting songs of patriotism and love in the classrooms.
Mothers and fathers agile in the buzzing markets for what theirs will eat.
Teachers going to school, with their heads high,
neatly dressed to fill the vessels with knowledge
And mold lives into forms of pillars to the nation.
I stare, totally amazed, totally in awe and love for my land.

Then Boom!!
The rain poured like never before, the thunder rumbled in anger
And the lights went out, leaving us in the silent dark.
As I wake up in the cold morning
To loud and terrifying sounds never before heard.
I peeped out through the window and my heart bled
As I see my brothers hustling on the streets, holding guns.
My other brothers whom I admired so much
in their commanding attire who once defended us from enemies outside,
now pointing their guns at our very own.

So, I take another walk through the streets and behold!
The schools are deserted, the markets are empty, the streets are quiet
All I hear are loud sounds of cries and anguish and pain
Mothers holding the cold bodies of their children to their

bosom drenched in their blood.
Cries of misery all around. My little babes can no longer chant
The stench of death hovering around
The stench of burning flesh, the stench of blood is heavy in the air.
Laughter has run out the door and we are not sure when it's coming back.
Death has made a bed in our homes and we are not sure when it is leaving either.
All I hear are the drums of war, beating from afar.
All I see is the gnashing of teeth; we feed on our tears daily.
Yet nobody hears us, we look from afar anxiously for help, but none forthcoming.

I cry for my land, my once beautiful
Now in shambles
I cry for peace; I pray the guns will go silent again
I pray the love, peace, and harmony will reign again.
This is the cry of a sister.

Mundi Prisca Ewonkem

Our Childhood of Memories

Standing in here it seems grandma is telling me a story of the
evils of conflict, but no it's a reality and not a story.
I am living the pain of war.
Here I am standing in our burnt house with my eyes wide
open looking at the frustrated future and confused tomorrow
all covered in fear, trauma, and pain.
And I heard a voice saying "don't worry it will get better"
"How better?" I asked when all my childhood stories must
have turned into nightmares, wait ohh!
Do I even have joyful childhood stories to tell and with
whom will I share the stories, when every day one soul goes
untimely to the other world. And to think of it that I was
born during the war too.

Ohhhh how I wish I could enjoy childhood days with.
"Mami play play"
"Hide and seek" , all children's games in my community!
Behold, I am into this action movie.
I am living and witnessing the reality of gunshots, killings,
and the burning of houses as part two of the film.
Hmmmmm waiting for part three if and only if I won't be
dead at that time.
Is my coming to this world or getting into the womb of a
woman in anglophone Cameroon a crime?
So why then punish me with fear, sadness, pain, and trauma
as my childhood memories.
All I desire is for the guns to be silent
Please give us the chance to live in peace
Please give us the chance to enjoy our childhood memories
Please give us the chance to play and watch the sunset
Please give us the chance to dance under the moonlight

Please give us the chance to run home for mama's food
We want to go to school freely and return home excited
Show some sympathy and stop the killing
Show some respect for humanity and stop the violence.
My tiny little voice is all I have now.

Ndefon Beatrice

Let's Decide to Love

CAMEROON
The Africa in miniature,
The Triangle of Peace.
What has befallen you? You suddenly changed from green to
red!! Yes
The fertile breadbasket of Africa to her bloodily slain sons
and daughters.
Oh cry the beloved country.
2016, the lights went dim, and brothers seized to recognize
brothers.
2017, darkness fell, the shootings, the killings, beheading,
raping, and kidnapping.
2018, the third year, no school! the future leaders are illiter-
ates or are dead
2019, death, anger, hatred, the manipulation, the infighting
Tomorrow, bleak, dark clouds, sounds of iron, smoking bar-
rels, strife, hunger, death.
Enough!!! The time to change is now, let's start from a little
move.
Stop the noise. Silence the guns.
Let's deny to waste,
Let's deny Hate.

Foncha Anang Emmerencia
❀ ❀ ❀

Cry Our Beloved Students

We cry out to you oh commandeers.
We hope you restore our schools
Whatever you do for us
We do not want to be part of an illiterate generation.
We do not want to carry guns.
We just want you to understand us.

We cry out to you oh commandeers.
We need safe learning space.
We desire nonviolent alternatives
We demand for immediate ceasefire.
We want love not hate.
We bargain just for a peaceful learning community.

We cry out to you oh commandeers.
Where have you kept your values?
What about morals?
Which life's lessons are you teaching us?
Why do you generate so much violence?
Who is responsible for the excessive hate speech today?

We cry out to you oh commandeers.
We just want peace.
We just want love.
We just want happiness.
We just want education.
We just want your support.
We the students of today.
We need your support.

Foncha Anang Emmerencia

The Pathetic Face of the Anglophone Crisis

Let the world hear my story
A story about a senseless war.
One which brings untold sufferings
The ongoing war in the two English-Speaking Regions of
Cameroon.

Listen to me talk
About this pathetic conflict
Which leaves many in the bushes.
Young boys and girls
Fighting or hiding
No access to education
But for a bleak future.

Many more in town
Our cities heavily militarized
Armed fighters patrolling the neighborhood.
Two factions with diametrically opposed instructions
Leaving the people confused

Our people have been killed
Students and teachers maimed
Others raped
Property destroyed, IDPs everywhere
No one is free because everyone is a victim
We are not at all safe

Is it too much to ask for a ceasefire?
Who are they fighting for if they burn down our houses?
Who are they defending, if they instill fear in us?
Why are they fighting if they can't face each other at the

dialogue table?
How do we put an end to this calamity?

We all tell this tale differently
We blame some and hail some
We try to justify the unjustifiable
We think we are in control of the drama
But I tell you, no one can boast of safety.

Yes, I say no one
When they carryout mass burnings
When innocent people are kidnapped
When civilians are raided and arrested without crimes
When we are gruesomely maimed/ traumatized

Then we are left homeless
We cough out huge ransoms
We are taken and abandoned in prisons
Irrespective of the kind of prisons
With whoever as commander/ general

We are raided and looted
Even on Sundays
And in camps, we are disrespected and beaten.
Yes, even elderly persons
I wonder what cultural values for our new generation.

Tell me, how can we possess durable bliss?
When did we get off the track of true happiness?
How can innocent civilians pay a price so dear?
Well said, the fight between two elephants leaves the grass to
suffer.

We will survive
I believe we can solve this crisis
With God at the center
With SNWOT peace builders pointing to the right direction.

Beatrice Titanji

A Bargain... No! Never

We never bargained for this; but it came to us.
We never bargained for full-scale war.
It started like a joke
Excited kids threw stones with catapults
The men spun the kids in the game.
The kids' toys became deadly weapons; its effects they never
knew.
They took the weed, and the game became real.
They left the classrooms, barred them
Goats became students
Cane rats became discipline masters.
The snakes the guardians
Daring any human kid
The nightmare was not a dream
We struggle to wake up
We say it is just a dream.
But Alas! It's real, so real.
Shaken by a call
A mother is dead
As the kids are crying
"Mama! Mama!
Let's go, they're coming again"
And they come, like wounded lions
And yet we hope for another alive to be spared
Of a mother, to tell her story someday, somehow.

Beatrice Titanji

That Child

Yes, that child was born three years ago. I don't know him at all. His charred body online breaks my heart, Crime? Born at the wrong time, born in a strange village. All had turned strange.

He could barely speak when he faced adversity
Yes, adversity from those
Who had to hold his hand to help him grow into a man but no! no! no!
It cannot be, will never be
His dad's face is unknown to him.
'Cos his mom was raped
Now he lies bare-chested on the ashes of what was a home. Home?
Did he ever know or have a home anywhere? He's been in and out the forest severally. Could that have been home?
That child will never be there to tell us their story.
Their frightened charred face is online for the world to see. Who knows them? Maybe their mom but where's she? Back to the forest. The haters are still there fuming, looting and raping the women and the land itself.
Yes, that child has known no peace. Now they are at peace.

Gilian Ndikum
❀ ❀ ❀

Home, My Sweet Home!

Oh home! My sweet home, when shall I see thee again?
That home that gave me solace when I sought for one
That home where I took my annual, summer break and week-
end to rest in,
That home that once had peaceful, loving and sincere people,
That home where animals and birds woke me up in the
morning,
That home with plenty of milk and honey...

Oh, home sweet home
I can't climb the grass hills nor explore the tropical forest
I crave the serenity in this once peaceful home
Whispering with chirping birds and squealing monkeys
Which has become a total slaughterhouse
With crashing grating gunshots competing on whose sounds
loudest and slays most
Sad enough they are my own blood slashing each other apart
and inflicting untold suffering on us all.

Quietude, harmony, and love have all become alien now
And bushes are now home, and insects and animals our
neighbors
Our hearths now cold ashes and memories of the good old
days.
Now gunshots our wake-up cockerels.
I yearn for the warmth of the fire with corn roasting on the
coals

Ceasefire now!
Stop the guns!
Let's dialogue!

Sarah-Derval E. Lifanda
❀ ❀ ❀

The Pain

When laughter was an integral part of us,
When peace was all we knew and understood
Now we sit and mourn the loss of our loved ones,
We mourn our homelessness, our precipitated widowhood,
And yes, we mourn an unknown future.

Why? O why? Were we not warned of the wolves in sheep
clothing?
The pain, the egoism, the greed

Engineered by the hands of Evil,
The sounds of gunshots sweep off fond memories of laughter
Blowing it away as harmattan wind the footprints in dust
With the cold smoking steel, we are helpless
As we bear the brunt of all your trampling.

We cry, we lament as rivers overflow like the slaughterhouse
is upstream
As they again and again torch our homes
And take our maidens to the bushes
And rid them of their jewels
Violating their very sacredness
When youth mutate into scavenging predatory beasts
Our hearts are chopped into tiny bits,
And the pain sears through like vinegar in a sore.

May the smoking steels become pens
And the land healed of human lions.

Anonymous
❁ ❁ ❁

War, Oh War

I've heard and read about your ugly and horrific face.
Little did I know I could see and live with you in Ground
Zero.
War oh war!
Who invited you to this our once beautiful land of milk and
honey?
For how long are you going to stay again?

War oh War!
Are you not tired of separating us from our once united and
loving families?
Our streets are littered with cadavers for dogs and pigs to
prey on.
Yet no one cares.
Where have you kept your consciences?

War Oh War!
You are manipulative, frightened by all, young or old, in uni-
form or not.
Suspicions of "climb bike" torture, murder, ransom fills the air.
Who is the enemy here?

War oh War!
Our streets have become desolate.
Gatherings, gossip, and laughter have disappeared from our
road junctions.
We have stopped hearing the cries of babies and birds have
ceased to sing their sweet melodies at dawn.

War oh War!
GZ has been abandoned to the old to fend for themselves.

Are they widows, widowers, childless or without relations?
No! Their offspring are lamenting in the bushes, foreign lands
and some in the pit of hell.
Old people now live like newly wedded couples seeking the
fruit of the womb.

War oh War!
Where are our scholars?
School premises have been deserted.
Our baby girls have been transformed to mothers.
Our education basket has been clamped down. Knowledge
has migrated to the West.
Saddened and weary, mothers pull their progeny from one
direction to another, Searching for education.
Misery, desperation, sickness, and poverty are now our bread.

War, you are evil!
Leaders, stop the war!
Stop shooting and killing.
Lay down your arms.
Stop burning and destroying property, lifelong investment!
End hostilities
Men, Women, Youths join us to shout for peace to return.
We need peace!
Let love lead!

Angeline Doh
❀ ❀ ❀

The Internally Displaced! My Little Story

In my own very land, I am internally displaced.
I laughed when I heard the phrase IDP not knowing I was
not far from being one.
Because of the Anglophone crisis, many things have hap-
pened to me.
My daughter was kidnapped in exchange for a ransom.
My business shut down, my home abandoned!
I am now an IDP wandering from one place to another.
Home is home!
Stop the war!

Josephine Yelang
❋ ❋ ❋

A Letter to God: From a Disheartened Cameroonian Daughter

Father God, Almighty Creator, God of war and peace, King and Majesty, Conqueror and God over all the universe. Father I am sending YOU this letter because I am disheartened and devastated by happenings in my land and don't know where else to turn to...

You are our strong tower to whom we run and are safe... Papa I am hurt, I'm totally confused by all around me. I got up this morning Lord and remembered how great a nation you built Cameroon and made it a Fatherland, a land of promise, a land of glory.... It was so wonderfully made that all proudly called it " Africa in miniature" and it was known for peace, works and, of course, a Fatherland to all...

Father God, then the devil saw that it was good and came walking, knocking, lulling and planting seeds of manipulation, marginalization and humiliation; causing division and assimilation; brainwashing and enslaving the spirit of our people...

As if that was not enough Lord, he injected demons of mass destruction and since 2016, the dark clouds of evil and weapons of mass destruction have covered the face of our land Cameroon with death and pain

God, what went so badly wrong that you turned your back on your own? Can't we fix it by your mercy and grace, Papa? Your innocent lives are falling, blood bath is feeding the demons; the tempest of war is raging and the innocent are suffering and dying...

Father, women, mothers and girls from South West and

North West wailed and lamented; spoke to Government leaders; spoke to the Pro-independent fighters as their mothers, sisters, wives and daughters...; sought help everywhere to no avail....

Father God, when I saw Ivory Coast fighting one brother against the other and South Africans killing their African brothers and chasing them away, I said to myself, "this is crazy, brothers can't do that to each other"...!!! Father, what do I tell the world is happening to my country Cameroon today? How did we get here? Love for worldly power, wealth, fame, territory and position? Where has the love for our fellow countrymen, women, children, brothers, sisters, parents eclipsed to?

Father God, in 2019 my newly orphaned cousin was shot with her daughter on her way to bury her dead husband in the North West. It felt like a nightmare.... As my tears were about to dry off that week, I heard gun shots in the early mornings around my neighborhood that burst in the air like popcorn... Terrified, my family and I dove for safety on the floor and on getting up, our neighbor had been taken away and brought back as a corpse the following day...
Father Lord, that same week, my uncle and wife were shot in the village in the North West by their own brothers, in front of their 5-year-old grandson who ran into the bushes in terror... Papa, such are stories from the South West and North West since 2016

Lord God, tears, tears, tears, fears and pain are all we have left. Our children whose diapers we changed with love and whom we hugged with lullabies to sleep; whom we fed and happily accompanied to school now point guns and rattle venomous words against their families....
Lord, where did your children go wrong? Can't we fix it by your mercy and grace Lord?

Father God, you said to David that the battle is of the Lord....You are God that does not slumber nor sleep. Papa, this is a cry of distress from a disheartened Cameroonian daughter... Lord, we are more than hopeless in the face of this situation where your children are innocent, armless yet victims of cold-blooded murder; the blood of your creation spilt in public no longer means a thing to our leaders; even the international community acts as spectators as lives languish in mass destruction; hospitals, homes, schools, chiefdoms, all destroyed... Father God, would you also stay silent?

Father God, may I please ask this question even though you say we shouldn't question you... Would a Leader of a country truly organize an election if his wife, daughter, son, mother or father were killed and his house burnt or his family helplessly sent to the bushes by gun men? Papa God, is the solution to this crisis burning of houses and killing innocent souls? God, Your people are helpless and confused in the face of this man-made catastrophe to which our leaders appear so indifferent. Papa God, please, come to our aid; touch the hearts of our President, ministers and the Pro-independent fighters...; Papa touch their hearts; let them know that we all are your creatures; that they can dialogue; that the innocent lives of Cameroonians and their blood belong to you; that they are called to protect the people and not to destroy them; that as leaders they are called to be humble, to listen to one another, to serve and not to be served ; that the lives of their sons, daughters, brothers, sisters, fathers and mothers whom they have all refuged safely abroad are as important as that of the poor and innocent dying every day in the South West and North West; that the disabled and old people are also Cameroonians; that we all need to feel at home in our country; to be loved equally; to benefit from the wealth on equal terms; that we also like to spend our country's money and enjoy life the way they and their children, families and friends do; that we want peace and tranquility too; that we deserve to be happy too....

Papa God, I know you are hearing my pleas; I know you are a God of justice and grace; please don't be silent on Cameroon anymore.
Papa God, despite the Grand National Dialogue since 2019, no concrete results have been implemented like ceasefire... please, God of Moses, Abraham and Jacob, please, speak to the storms of war in our land; please arrest the guns and let there be #CEASEFIRE; #PEACE we need...

Please God, render the arms that carry the guns inactive and the powers that fuel the war weak for the sake of peace. We can only move on socially, politically, economically and religiously strong if and only if there is humility, love, honesty, true dialogue with all and peace.

Father God, please impact our leaders with the fear of the Lord, wisdom and humility to sit down as children of Cameroon and have honest conversations about this issue. They know the root causes, they know the truth, they know the solutions; Father arrest our leaders with humility; wash pride away from them, let them stop thinking arrogantly and start thinking and honestly talking peace for the sake of innocent lives Papa
You did it in Rwanda, yes Lord you will do it in Cameroon Father God.
Papa, capture our land with grace, please Lord...

With much appreciation, thank you Father, thank you Lord...
Your Daughter

Germaine Njeh
❋ ❋ ❋

Restore our Bread Basket

I am a farmer in misery because of this war
I can no longer access most of my farmlands
For fear of being kidnapped, arrested or killed
Even those I managed to cultivate, I am unable to harvest
Some of the produce I harvest, there are no buyers
Those who manage to buy pay relatively low prices
I am unable to repay the loan I took to buy farm inputs

The Micro finance institution is after me to recover the loan
but I have nothing to offer
The collateral security, my house has been burned and I am
homeless
My teenage daughters have gotten pregnant
My sons now fight against each other forgetting that we are
all God's creatures
Tears have become my breakfast, lunch and supper
When will all this end? Where did we go wrong?

I toiled day and night on my farm to educate you
Today some of you are Ministers, Activists, Lawyers, Doctors,
Professors, Pastors, Job seekers etc.
You take decisions without considering the repercussions on a
poor farmer like me.
Is this how you wish to repay me for making sure that you are
'big men' with authority today?
Is this the pay for making steady your food supply in the best
quality always?

Our homes have been burnt with some of us in it
Our animals also killed, property have been looted
Our storehouses are burnt with our harvest inside

Our people now live in constant fear of the unknown
Our days have become gripped by uncertainty
Our children, brothers, husbands, fathers and sisters, when
will all these stop?

Keep your pride and let there be a ceasefire
We are tired and we know, you are tired too
Peace is what we crave for, justice is what we need
We can once more stand side by side to fight for a better
course

Let's build our land from its ashes to beauty again
Please, restore our breadbasket.

Beatrice Akwe Afon Tamilo

Sacrificed Generations

A generation sacrificed at the altar of the mighty greedy gods.
We are now foreigners to peace.
The gods of our land are at a tug-of-war and we the grass are
suffering.
How can this generation have peace without justice.
Sleep evades us because of the sound of guns. Thunder in the
heart of the dry harmattan breeze.

OMG save us from our sons, brothers, nephews and hus-
bands.
Save us from the greedy gods who are chasing us and burning
our abodes and making us kin to those animals our Creator
made us shepherds over.
Why all the fighting?
Why all the killings?
Why? Why? Why?
Listen to the voice of reason: both of you are WRONG.
Give this generation a chance.

Clotilda Andiensa
❀ ❀ ❀

Resilience in Adversity

In the face of adversity
warriors are united in diversity
Of continuous shameless criminality
Albeit in all sorts of Atrocities
Looting and raping, You're all guilty

Right, a promise of a bright future
Left, a promise of protection and defense
A promise to resist
A promise to crush
We, TOYS of promises without consent

To uphold your promises
The competition is high
You salute with the guns
And smile at your brothers' corpses
You are all guilty

Of burning down villages
Is it reconstruction?
kidnapping for ransom
Is it the better future?
Our pain is your joy
You are all guilty

I am a woman peace builder
In the heat of adversity
I choose to be positive
I choose to be tolerant
I rise up to speak for the voiceless

I am a woman peace builder
I am your mother
I live with a disability
I am your wife, I am pregnant
I am your daughter, I long to go to school.

Akwo Eileen
❀ ❀ ❀

Dark Clouds Cover the Land

Ring it in, ring it in, ring in songs of woe
Beat the drums, beat the drums, let the tears begin to flow
All around, all around, all around tears rolling down
Up above, up above, up above dark clouds come tumbling on

Dark clouds in the morning
Dark clouds when we're mourning
Dark clouds in our moaning
Dark clouds we are done in

There you stand holding the gun
Like the old man's son John
There you stand carrying the fire
Burn, burn, burn, you conspire

Yeah, you say we are done in
Yeah, you say you have done it

As the fire rages on
As the smoke rises up
As the clouds begin to form
On the morrow dark clouds will come

So, we say our voice is strong
Though we mourn the songs roll off our tongue
In this land where we belong
Where we'll stay and be strong.

Clementina Njang Yong

A Cry for Help

My beloved coastal region of the Southwest.
My cherished mountainous highlands region of the North-
west.
The two regions where life has always been the best.
But now our patience has been put to the test.
As our continuous plea for a ceasefire has not been put to
rest.
Yet, our cry for peace is incessantly our quest.

Many have taken the last resort to flee to the West Region.
The underprivileged, however, are condemned to build their
nests,
And camp with unfamiliar creatures like unwanted guests.
In bushes where they are exposed to all pests.
As only a few were lucky to escape with their vests.
Who says this scenario is just a jest?

It has been a long scary dream.
The lights are dim.
Everywhere is filled with gloom.
And there is no single face with a grin.

When the sounds started we were asleep.
I woke up to find no one around the hearth.
With my weak and tiny little feet,
I was able to run away from the heat.

And now I cry out with all my might.
I am filled with a lot of fright.
And I wonder if my future will ever be bright,
When all I have lived for, dreamt of has been burnt down in

a night.

Who will hear my tiny little voice?
Do you think I am just making noise?
Do you think my cry is not worth your intervention?
Do you think I am one of those "Boys"?

Please let it be worthy of your note;
I am just a vulnerable victim, still filled with hope.
By His grace I know I will be able to cope.
Even as you decide to look away during my distress call for
your help.

Omam Esther
❀ ❀ ❀

Who am I?

Seating on the mountain, listening to the sweet sound of
breeze,
I heard a voice asking- Who are you?
And I replied,
I am a child of the mountains, hills and valleys
I am a child of the farms and palm plantations
I am a child of banana and rubber plantations
I am a child of Ndu and Tole tea.
I am a child of the labor and struggles of my parents
I am a child of the toils that they underwent for us
They always told us that education is power,
They always told us that education is the future of every
nation
They always told us; my child, do not play with your educa-
tion
Yes, they always told us they will go hungry for us to go to
school
What happened to that promise?
All we hear nowadays is the sound of machine guns
All we feel is never ending fear
Amor cars have invaded the land
Ambushing all that stand in their way
They fall in their numbers left and right
Things have fallen apart – don't you see?
Where is your promise? When would I go to school?
When would I become that promised future?
No playing in the fields nowadays, where are my parents?
Hear my cry, see my tears and pains?
Who am I? All I hear day and night – the sounds
Boom, boom boo, kakakakakakak boom
How can you watch such slaughter and be calm? Not moved?

Who am I?
To whom shall I turn to? Ooooh my home my home, when
shall I see my home again?
Who am I?
I am now a child of the Slums, A child of the streets,
I now live in uncompleted buildings, I now live on the streets,
Market stalls, petrol stations, bridges
I am a homeless, fatherless and motherless child
My dreams – shattered, my life in shamble,
My only daily aim is to survive, and hopefully to return home
at night.
School is good for others not for me?
Schools are safe for others, but not for me
They now use me for their games- Who am I?
I am not my problem, I am not my illiteracy,
They forced it on me because I am a child of the war zones
Yet, I am not my problem, because THEY ARE.

Chambi Julie
❀ ❀ ❀

The Nightmare Turns Real!

It's about 7am. It's a bright day. I'm supposed to be out already. No! I am in. Gunshots I hear from every side. I hear you could distinguish the gunshots, but can I? No, I am just scared. I hear the rooms are not safe. Can we try the corridors? Yes, we can. The children are there already. So, there is the school for the young ones. The streets are deserted. The school gates and classes are locked too! Another teacher and student have just been kidnapped. The sound of the once welcome "Okada" sends us running. But where to? Towards the road to the armored cars with its fierce-looking occupants. Can we run again? No! Can we stand still? No! Either way we are as good as dead. So, the dead toll increased on the streets, then in the homes, then to the bushes.

O God! the village has cast out her youth! All the young men are gone! Some to the world beyond, others to the dirty street corners of some far away town. Are they safe? Safe you say? And the young girl? What awaits her? Rape, unwanted pregnancy, Sexually Transmissible Infections that will not heal for the hospitals have been burnt down, no doctors, some too have been kidnapped and some chased out from there. Then I was taken through the dead town with overgrown bushy footpaths and village streets. Even the bridge too has been broken.

The women, the children, the old men, and people living with disabilities are trapped! There is bad news in the village. The houses have been burnt down! The animals too; even the fowls have been killed! We must run to the bushes our only hope! Here we are in the bushes even in the heart of the rains and the scorch of the dry season sun. Are we safe from bush fires? The voice of women in labor is heard in the bushes, the shrill voice of newborn babies crying for help. Will someone help!

Kate Tande
❀ ❀ ❀

The Groaning of an Anglophone Child

I am a child, I am an innocent being. I don't deserve to be raised in an unhealthy context.
Our schemas are already adjusted to the sights and sounds of gunshots
The burnings, the killings, the kidnappings, the hostilities, hate language and the vices.
We are now fatherless, motherless or totally orphaned - oh what a world. What early experiences will back us up in the future. We need to bond, be loved, cared for like other children.
The schools, our religions, the safe neighborhoods, communities have been polluted. How do we imbibe the values, norms, mores that held us together? We are indeed traumatized by hostilities mediated through our parents and caregivers... Our major support system. Our rights to basic needs trampled and justice is sometimes blind.

Yes, we are the pillars of tomorrow, the pride and heritage of our parents. We are the proof of fatherhood and motherhood amidst the noise and hate. In our parenting and child rearing, we keep the faith, hope and resilience for the best which is yet to come. We have a right to blossom in a threat-free context. No to violence. The African child, the Cameroonian child, the Anglophone child deserves holistic development. We need an enabling environment where we can have access to education, health and necessities for our well-being. Our physical, cognitive, socio-emotional, spiritual and cultural developmental needs must never be compromised. We cry for justice, we cry for sustainable peace.

Zoneziwoh Mbondgulo-Wondieh

We Survive

Woke up and asked myself
What I will do
When that day comes
When all this is over
When we all shall sing and say
At last - We survived.

We survived the stray bullets
We survived the incarceration
We survived the brutality
We survived famine
We survived the pains and thoughts of never knowing what's
next
We survived the random arrests
We survived the sickness
We survived the hiding
We survived.

At last - we survived
Come dear all
Party with me
Even as the tears will never dry off my eyes
Come
Come party with me
It's been long because
We survived.

We survived
Now - I can cook once more at my veranda like my great
granny used to do
We survived

Now, I will tie my loincloth around my chest like the old days and walk the hallway of my front yard like models of Broadway

Oh yes - we SURVIVED
Now, I will eat outside and call all to serve themselves from the pot
Because I know, they like me - we survived.

Beatrice Manka Atanga

Peace

Peace rarer than a dog's tear
Peace, an image log forgotten
Peace, the illusionary abundance of silent thunder
Peace the abundant quiet of explosive pistons
Peace the bloodied streams on the streets
Peace the cacophonous streets at midday
Peace, the burnt shelters sending wrinkled mothers crouching
in the bushes
Peace the mirage that once was
Peace, the hope that hangs on every tongue.

Beatrice Manka Atanga
❀ ❀ ❀

The Wrong Way

The river that now flows upwards
With its waters red, spews frightful creatures
Its fish is poison, as it swims and drinks the crimson opiate
How did all these begin?
The springs meant to quench the thirst
Corrodes the throat
The thunder that brings rain now rumbles from a pipe
And smokes its fumes of acid
And its lightning strikes without discrimination
And like cockroaches, its victims lie waste.

Etengeneng Arrey
❀ ❀ ❀

A Strange Knock

A Strange Knock I heard
I was shocked with what I saw
A quick prayer I said.

The gun shots were loud and heavy
The screams were loud and deafening.

The sky was dark.
The birds stopped singing.
The toads and frogs disappeared.
The women were stranded.
The markets were deserted.
The schools were shut down.
The hospitals and homes burnt.

Jennet Sesighe

Round on the Beautiful Table we Sat

All day, all-night; year in, year out
With abundance of food, abundance of water
We ate, we drank with thankfulness to God
In our beautifully designed uniforms we matched freely to
school
Morality and social norms guarded our way
Cleanliness, determination and hard work were a part of us
Our teachers were our mini gods
We were admired and called peaceful
Until that Day.

That Day, O that Day
They rumored, they whispered
The clouds gathered, the sun stood still
The sound of the gun filled the air
The streets deserted, the markets deserted
Our citadel of learning grows thorns
And our brothers were radicalized
That which we were never permitted to watch on TV, we
watched live
Torture, killings, non-respect filled our land
Our brothers, our fathers, our sisters murdered in cold blood
We wailed, we mourned, we prayed
Our churches gathered, our priest led prayers, our mothers
lamented, our youths matched
Yet nothing changed

That Day, O that day
We found ourselves in a strange land
We got new names (IDPs, Refugees), we resisted yet that was
our new status

Then the reality of no house, no food, no water hit us
We became beggars on the streets, our bodies violated for a
loaf of bread...
Where did we go wrong?
God where are You!

Ekoume Ndema Irene

Oh God, we need You more than Yesterday

Have we failed to seek Your face Lord?
Have we depended on our own efforts and wisdom and
thought we can do it without You?
Are we being punished for our wickedness and selfish interest
exhibited even in the process of peace building and obtaining
justice?
Are we being punished because we are not true to ourselves?
A lot of hypocrisy and suspicion has enveloped us.
Are we being punished because we went for *odeshi*
Rather than crying out to You like the Israelites did in
Egypt?
The *odeshi* has failed us, the Government has failed, even the
UN and other peace-building institutions seem lost.
No one seems to know what to do.
Efforts are made but the crisis keeps escalating.
See how people die every day.
See how property gets destroyed every day.
Don't even know what tomorrow holds for us.
Almighty God, Mighty Man in battle, you who knows the
end of a thing from its beginning, we need You more than
yesterday.
Intervene in our land Lord...
We are in tears and in pains.

Anonymous
❀ ❀ ❀

Our Tears

We called for a dialogue with our tears
We had the dialogue with hopes to dry off our tears
We believed in the outcome of the dialogue so that there will
be no more tears

A peace caravan came along promising us all is well so there
will be no tears
In the traditional speech we were again reassured that elec-
tions will mark the end of our tears
Yes, elections will come with total protection and new leaders
that there will be no need for our tears.

I can say there were promises, wishes or dreams
We have known real violence that we wish were only dreams
Our houses burnt, we are living in the bushes or fleeing for
safety and all our faces bathed in our tears
Humans are now slaughtered and roasted like chicken and
goats so we can't control our tears

Women let's dry up our tears
Let's face our fears
Let's tell our stories loud and clear so that everyone hears.

Delphine Mbongue

Oh, My Homeland

A land of plenty,
A land of fullness, a land of adequacy,
A land of abundance.
What have u turn into?
Oh my homeland:
No more shelter, No more refuge, No more commonality.
No more dining and winning together!

Oh my homeland,
where do l run to from here?
What happened to the beautiful moments we all shared as
siblings from same womb?
What went wrong that we can't see face to face again?
What happened that we now fight and kill each other?
What happened that our children are homebound for years!

Ooh my homeland,
Where I looked forward to spend vacation to get relief from
the hustle and bustle of the city.
What do l meet there? Flames but not from the cooking in
the kitchen,
Ashes but not from firewood,
Strange perfume in the air...not from roasted crickets but
my burnt children, sisters and brothers, mothers, fathers and
grannies....
As I scream in despair all I get is the echoes of my own
screaming,

Oh my homeland;
Neighbourhood transformed to cemetery with graves as
homes.

Oh my homeland,
Oh God our refuge.
Strangers have invaded my sweet homeland.

Lilian Atanga
❀ ❀ ❀

Na Weti Dis Eh?

Chai!! Weti person don do
How dem fit burn man laka frawood
Wusai ancestor dem go eh
Wusai da tunda wey wi bi know
Today we need wunna
Wusai kibaranko
Wusai mabu
Wusai chong
Kwifo u lep ya pikin dem for who
Chai!! Or na ekelebe or na amba dem oh
Weti man e pikin do
Even ngrumbib no di die so
A beg or na ndepende or na weti oh
Wuna lib pipos dem pikin dem
Wuna cari boretic leave ma pipo
Cra don finish fo ma ai
Dem di laf me now so
Shame don pass me
Vex don pass me
Cra don pass me.

Lilian Atanga

My Dignity, My Pain

They came at 3am
Knocked at my door.
Again the usual way
I was alone
Frightened
I remembered
It was only last week
On the way to the farm
That I bore the shame of a woman
That my laps were peeled
Splintered like a log of wood
By a ferocious beast
Whose gun poked my sides
My me-ness invaded
Leaving me dripping red, crawling, crying till I got home
Home I thought was sanctuary
It is a week today
Locked in here
Preserving the little
Of the violated garden left
Hiding sores on my spirit
Again, they jammed the door
Once broken before
A searing light into my face
A voice from the deep
'Choose me or death'
I had no choice
He made it for me
My fruits harvested again
Beaten with a stick with thorns
tearing the ripened glow

A rot engulfed me
Again, he shredded the mango
Poisoning it with his rotten teeth
As he plunged into its once tainted juiciness
And my spirit he took
For only pulp was left
Because me
Like my sisters
Have lost it
Our dignity
Has become our pain.

Lilian Atanga
❀ ❀ ❀

Let it Shine

When pain is beyond tears
When it numbs feelings
And stalls thinking
When there is no more rhyme or reason
When humanity is debased beyond animals
We must not give up
For even when there is only one soul
One that can still reason
One that is still human
One that cries out for help
We don't give up on it
For it takes only one lit candle
To light the others
Let us dig deep
And bring out that shard of light
To dissolve the darkness that engulfs us
Let's each say...
This little light of mine
I'm gonna make it shine.

Lilian Atanga

❀ ❀ ❀

Our Bodies, our Pain

Our pain our portion
Battered for our being
They turn us against us
They make us eat each other
Our blood becomes our wine
Our flesh our food
They make us relish in it
Believing we are fighting the enemy
When indeed the enemy laughs at us
Mocks us, humiliates us, and kills us
Their dungeons our homes and graves
Their smoking guns our gory music
Our women, our bodies, their crime scene
The playground of the boys in boots
Whose filthy masculinities feed on
Powerless as they are, the turn to the weak
And womanhood becomes a weapon of war
Pistons which know no bounds
And poke any sacred caves they find
Violating the very gods they once served
We are tired, our tears are dry
We stand up against violence on our people
We stand up for justice
We stand up for peace
We rise beyond the jungle.

Baiye Frida Ebai
❀ ❀ ❀

From Peace Plants to Blood

Trapped in a senseless war
Blood from punctured bodies fallen
War merchants thirsty for the wetness of blood
To bank as civilians sink into the hollowness of death
When will they stop and think Peace again?

Trapped into a web of hatred and greed
Blood money from war merchants
Hiding behind dove-like initiatives
Building blind lights with half truth
Will they think of the sweetness and light of Peace again?

Trapped into believing we can do better
Than the war merchants
Void of hatred and oppression in ideology
Amid conflicting selfish parties
Will they stop to think Peace in their eyes of greed?

Trapped in their darkness of manipulation
As the lights darkened
Let's try to find each other again
To construct peace, to reconcile
To let go of the pains of war
Will they stop to think Peace amid their violent response?

Are we too trapped in this vice?
Are women Peace-builders far from this fox-like hunt?
It's time to give back the value of our Peace Plants
To restore lost dignity and sisterhood
Can we stop to think genuine Peace again?

Mariana Ewokem

How we Got There

It started like a child's play
many were excited for change
They cheered them on
Hiding them from their enemies.

suddenly the tides turned
darlings became enemies
Confused and angry
they asked
How did we get here
These are not our darlings
yes! Those are your darling cubs
They now feed on your flesh.

There is still hope in the horizon
For you and your darling cubs.
They understand you.
They still love you their fatherland.

Louisa Tangie
❁ ❁ ❁

Blood on the Streets

The fear is crucial when citizens are forced to take sides,
to answer the questions, who is "good?" who is "evil?"
Children wide-eyed, and confused,
Women tortured and abused.
Come and see the blood in the streets

How do people recuperate from the devastating effect of the
crisis?
Especially as their homelands have been ravaged.
Wish I could express the emotions I feel,
So much misery, so much pain,
Come and see the blood in the streets

I'm frightened and scared,
for my life, the lives of the vulnerable,
We crawl, aimed at, and routinely killed,
No human being, such a death deserves
Come and see the blood in the streets

I see children and a crying wife,
Someone please stop them, from taking more lives.
We are tired, we are weak
God come to our rescue
Come and see the blood in the streets

Let's work on finding solutions,
let's meet at the dialogue table.
Hatred and anger, we must decrease,
Only path to finding peace.

Awah Francisca M
❀ ❀ ❀

Evasive Peace

As A Peace Advocate, Be Not Proud
Evasive Peace, Be not proud
That world's entire wealth can't purchase you.
Perhaps you could have been bought for Silver, Gold, Sapphires, Pearls and Diamonds too.
But dare you say, for LOVE you won't be sold?

Evasive Peace, be not proud
That high you dwell, atop a towering tor!
Like Bruce's spider, ceaselessly we will
Try to heave ourselves right up to your door
By scaling, inch by inch, your craggy hill!

Evasive Peace, be not proud
That none can see or hear you; so no clue
We have to track you down. But we can feel
Your presence versus present absence too
Suffices this, your hide-out to reveal!
Evasive Peace, Be not proud
That you, can keep mocking
Your chasers all for whom you're much too fast!
With 'golden apples', win we shall, at last!

Eteki Stella Dopgima

If only I could pick up the Pieces of their Lives

If only I could pick up the pieces of their lives
I would mend them together
The disruption, pain, changes of course, uncertainty, sorrow,
agony
Once upon a time happy, family striving for daily bread sud-
denly crushed
They came with guns and time stopped!
Father is nowhere to be found, brother hiding in bush, baby
crying on mother's back
Running to only the gods know where,
In the confusion, commotion bullet sounds fill the air, dark
clouds gather.
They've fled their homes, their only comfort zones but they
got here
Battered, worn out and tired.
Starved for days, barely drank any water
These are the stories I hear every day, there are even worse
scenarios
They keep me on my feet, at night I toss and turn
Sometimes crying on my knees for supernatural help to come
Thinking, strategizing how more can I be of help? How did
we get here?
I did not choose this path; it chose me that is why I keep
fighting
Their cries are mine; it could be me too
They've become my friends, even family
I see the strength in their smiles; admire the hope in their
eyes, truth on their lips
I hug and tell them, it ain't over
Let's see where tomorrow goes!
There is hope in the horizon.

Sally Mboumien
❀ ❀ ❀

Was it a Mistake?

They said they were fighting for us, and we believed
We believed every promise made was full of promises of care,
concern, and a good life for all
That now it seems, was not part of the plan
Part of the plan? Were (women), children, the elderly, and
Persons Living with Disabilities ever a part of it?
They said we were vulnerable
That we needed change.

Change? Was this the change we wanted?
Here we are homeless, in the bushes with hunger staring at
us.
Pain and suffering have become our portion thus increasing
caregiving needs.
Was it a mistake to be who we are?

Was it a mistake to believe and hope for a better life?
Was it a mistake to support, advise and lobby the leaders?
Was it a mistake to allow them to lead us?
Was it a mistake to call for an end to hostilities and an inclu-
sive and sincere dialogue?

Sally Mboumien
❀ ❀ ❀

Deep Regrets

If we knew we would have talked to each other
If we knew we would have gone to the dialogue table
If we knew we would have compromised for the sake of humanity

Now we have lost thousands to violence
Now we have hundreds of thousands displaced and living in misery
Now we have suspicion, betrayal, pain and bitterness residing within us
Now we have a stalemate

Why don't we talk to each other?
Why don't we move to the dialogue table now?
Why don't we do all to prioritize humanity?
Are all these years not enough?

Sally Mboumien
❀ ❀ ❀

Why?

I have heard people crying and sympathizing
I have heard different institutions and organizations make a
statement
I have heard justifications and explanations from various
factions
I have heard different calls for justice

All is not well from every indication
All is not well in the land
All is not well with the leaders of the various factions
All is not well with women and children as well as everyone

Does the situation in Rwanda years ago mean anything to us?
Does September 11th in the USA speak to us?
Does the Ngarbuh massacre resonate with you as a leader?
Does the mass offered in memory of the Valentine's Day
Massacre victims mean justice?

Why the silence from many activists and opinion leaders?
Why the open call for an investigation from some authorities
with no timelines or commitment?
Why the attempt to let time pass so that we forget this great
injustice?
Justice must be served. Investigate the Ngarbuh massacre for
it is too much.

Lilian Atanga
❀ ❀ ❀

Epilogue

Even when they wailed on the streets
Tore their clothes and walked naked
Shouted on the TV stations and radio shows
And even when they howled like wounded lions
And the social media almost spat them out

And even when they lost their sons, husbands and brothers
And their laps got peeled and invaded over and over again
And their children crushed like ripe red grapes
And their crimson juices spewing and painting the streets

Into a decade the pain remains
Into a decade the waiting and howling continues
Into a decade no one listens
And into a decade the crushing goes on.

ACKNOWLEDGEMENT

We want to acknowledge all the suffering women of the Southern Cameroons irrespective of color, creed, language, or ethnicity, and who have, in one way or the other, borne the pain of the violent, deadly and traumatic conflict.

We particularly want to acknowledge the vision bearer of the South West North West Women's Task Force, Ms. Esther Omam, for having the vision to create the platform for women and women leaders to come together to contribute to bringing sustainable peace in the South West and North West Regions. As the armed conflict rages on, the women are not giving up and continue to be foot soldiers to the needy and underprivileged, taking the frontlines in humanitarian activities as well as local peace initiatives.

We particularly acknowledge each and every member of the South West North West Women's Taskforce (SNWOT) for their unrelentless and continued engagement to the cause, and for contributing to this collection. We are proud of you all.

Finally, we want to thank every stakeholder who has supported the coalition both morally and financially.

And for those who do not trust us, we still thank you for your criticisms, give us feedback to improve.

Lilian Atanga & Sally Mboumien

ABOUT THE EDITOR

Credit: author

S ally Maforchi Mboumien is women, peace and security advocate, concerned citizen, teacher and feminist from Bawock, Cameroon. Sally has been working to uphold Sexual and Reproductive Health Rights (SRHR) especially for adolescent girls and young women in ways that can grant them access to decision-making spaces. Sally envisages a society void of inequalities and social injustices, where the ideals of feminism, freedom of expression and social inclusion are valued.

ABOUT THE EDITOR

Credit: author

Lilian Lem Atanga is an Associate Professor of Gender and Discourse Studies, formerly of the Department of African Studies of the University of Dschang, the University of Bamenda, and Fulbright Scholar at the University of Florida, USA. She is currently a senior research fellow at the University of the Free State, Bloemfontein, South Africa, and a senior consultant with North Highland Consulting. Since obtaining her PhD in Linguistics from Lancaster University, UK, she has researched on language, gender, politics and the media in African contexts. She has published books, chapters in edited volumes, and academic articles in high impact journals and encyclopedias. She's co-editor of *Gender and Language in Sub-Saharan Africa: Tradition, Struggle and Change* (John Benjamins 2013).

ABOUT THE PUBLISHER

Spears Books is an independent publisher dedicated to providing innovative publication strategies with emphasis on African/Africana stories and perspectives. As a platform for alternative voices, we prioritize the accessibility and affordability of our titles in order to ensure that relevant and often marginal voices are represented at the global marketplace of ideas. Our titles – poetry, fiction, narrative nonfiction, memoirs, reference, travel writing, African languages, and young people's literature – aim to bring African worldviews closer to diverse readers. Our titles are distributed in paperback and electronic formats globally by African Books Collective.

Connect with Us: Go to www.spearsmedia.com to learn about exclusive previews and read excerpts of new books, find detailed information on our titles, authors, subject area books, and special discounts.

Subscribe to our Free Newsletter: Be amongst the first to hear about our newest publications, special discount offers, news about bestsellers, author interviews, coupons and more! Subscribe to our newsletter by visiting www.spearsmedia.com

Quantity Discounts: Spears Books are available at quantity discounts for orders of ten or more copies. Contact Spears Books at orders@spearsmedia.com.

Host a Reading Group: Learn more about how to host a reading group on our website at www.spearsmedia.com

Printed in the United States
by Baker & Taylor Publisher Services